# JAMLO WALKS

## SAMINA MISHRA

### Illustrations by TARIQUE AZIZ

PUFFIN BOOKS

An imprint of Penguin Random House

It is day 7 of the lockdown

and everyone says the skies are blue again.

Jamlo walks.

She looks straight at the road ahead.
*It is long.*

The milestone says 'Nariapur 10'. Jamlo wipes the
sweat off her face and shifts the bag of chillis from
one shoulder to the other.

The chillis are what she earned for harvesting fields.

Jamlo knows Ma will be happy to see them.
She wishes she had earned more.
Last year Budhram Dada had returned
to Aaded with two sacks of chillis.

But Jamlo's work was cut short
and all she has is one cloth bagful.
Jamlo holds on to the bag and walks.

Amma is watching a video on the laptop of people w a l k i n g.
The news reporter's voice says something about Covid-19.

'...Four hours to prepare for a twenty-one-day lockdown...'

Tara sees men and women carrying bundles,
and children looking tired and sunburnt.

She has many questions. But when Amma notices
Tara, she quickly shuts the lid of the laptop.
The people walking disappear in a flash.

'Do you want dosa for breakfast?' asks Amma.

At the roadside stall, the man spreads
dosa batter on the tawa. It sizzles.
Jamlo watches.

The man asks her where she's coming
from and where she's going.

Jamlo likes that his eyes widen in amazement when she tells him.

'The road is long, walk with some grown-ups,'
the man says as he hands her a til ka laddoo from a glass jar.
Jamlo eats the laddoo as she walks past a turn-off that says **'Tadvai 15'**.

The road shimmers like water, empty of cars and buses.
She sees figures swaying in the shimmer.
Perhaps it is Hareli and everyone is dancing and eating laddoos.

Jamlo blinks.
A car with a flag roars down the road.

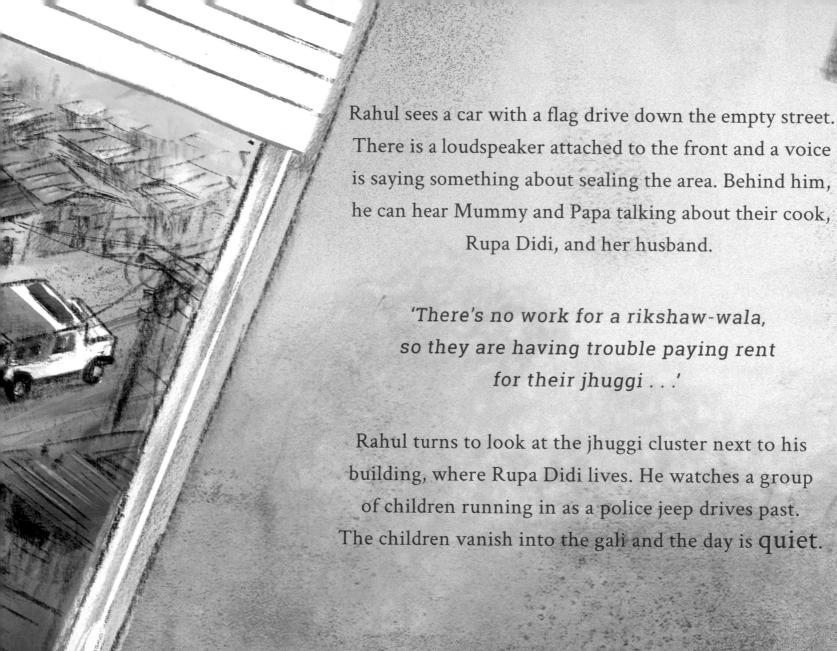

Rahul sees a car with a flag drive down the empty street.
There is a loudspeaker attached to the front and a voice
is saying something about sealing the area. Behind him,
he can hear Mummy and Papa talking about their cook,
Rupa Didi, and her husband.

'There's no work for a rikshaw-wala,
so they are having trouble paying rent
for their jhuggi . . .'

Rahul turns to look at the jhuggi cluster next to his
building, where Rupa Didi lives. He watches a group
of children running in as a police jeep drives past.
The children vanish into the gali and the day is quiet.

The silence on the road is
broken by the sounds of birds.
Jamlo sees a mynah drinking
from a puddle.

*Birds can't be locked down,*

thinks Jamlo.

But then she remembers the parakeet that Sarita had brought
home from the haat, and how they gave it guavas and
green chillis every day. She wonders if it is still in the cage.
The mynah twitters and looks at Jamlo.

Jamlo pulls out a dry red chilli from her bag and holds her hand out.
The bird flutters its wings and flies away. Jamlo puts the chilli
away and takes out her bottle of water that will soon be empty.
She squints her eyes, trying to see if she can spot a dhaba
or a village in the distance.

The road is still long and people are still w a l k i n g .

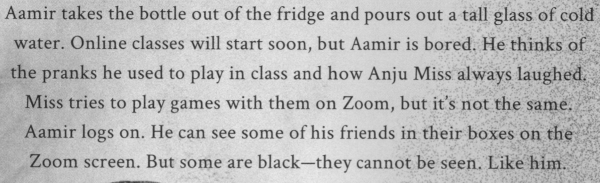

Aamir takes the bottle out of the fridge and pours out a tall glass of cold
water. Online classes will start soon, but Aamir is bored. He thinks of
the pranks he used to play in class and how Anju Miss always laughed.
Miss tries to play games with them on Zoom, but it's not the same.
Aamir logs on. He can see some of his friends in their boxes on the
Zoom screen. But some are black—they cannot be seen. Like him.

When Aamir complained, Papa said,
'At least you can hear. So many children
don't even have this . . .'

Aamir hears Anju Miss say *'Hi Aamir!'*
Then the sound becomes garbled and
the connection is broken.

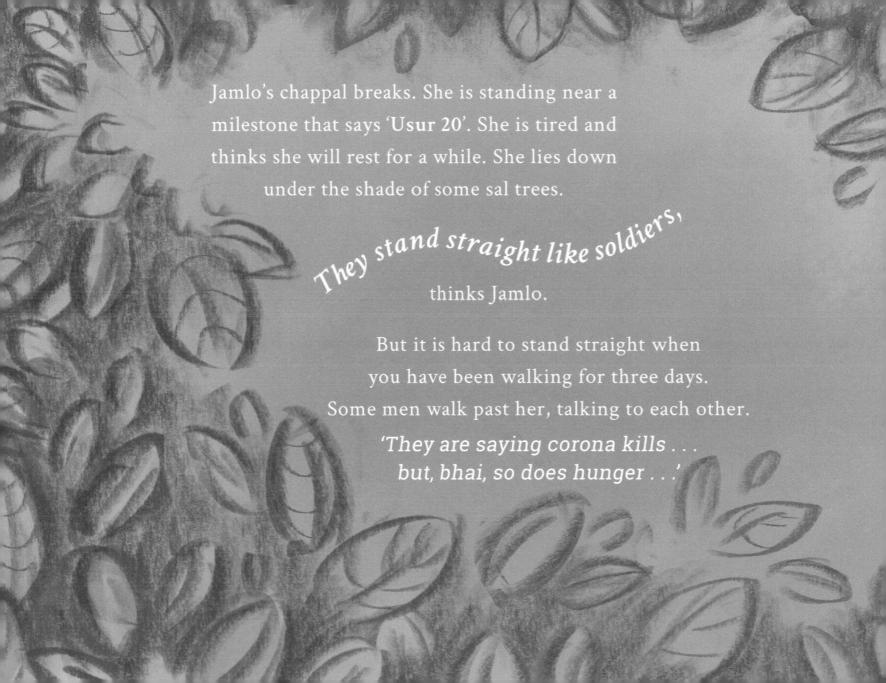

Jamlo's chappal breaks. She is standing near a
milestone that says 'Usur 20'. She is tired and
thinks she will rest for a while. She lies down
under the shade of some sal trees.

*They stand straight like soldiers,*

thinks Jamlo.

But it is hard to stand straight when
you have been walking for three days.
Some men walk past her, talking to each other.
*'They are saying corona kills . . .*
*but, bhai, so does hunger . . .'*

A leaf flutters down on to her face. Jamlo notices that it has turned partly yellow and knows that the tree has rejected it. She thinks of a 600-year-old tree growing somewhere in Bijapur that Pushpa Didi had told her about. She wonders how many leaves that tree must have rejected. And what it feels like to be that old.

Jamlo shuts her eyes.

She thinks of Ma and Bapu
and the chillis she will give them.
She thinks of how proud they will be
of how much she has walked.

It is morning.
Tara and Rahul and Aamir wake up to another day of online school.

Another day under lockdown rules.

The skies are still blue.

The road is still long.

The people are still w a l k i n g .

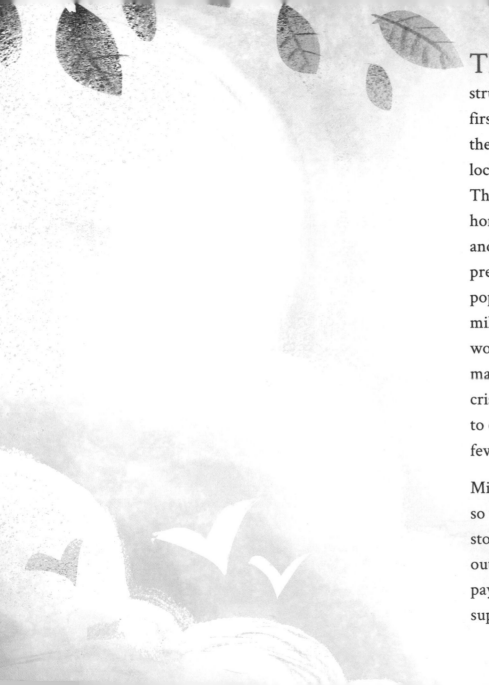

# The Covid-19 pandemic

struck the world at the end of 2019 and India had the first case at the end of January 2020. On 24 March, the government of India ordered a nationwide lockdown to stop the spread of coronavirus.

The people of India were ordered to stay in their homes, only venturing out to get essentials like food and medicine. They were given only four hours to prepare for a twenty-one-day lockdown. The entire population of the country was stunned and for the millions of Indians who build roads and buildings; work in homes, factories and fields; and live in makeshift settlements, this became an enormous crisis. These migrant workers are people who move to other places in search of work because there are few opportunities for them in their villages.

Migrant workers are mostly daily wage workers, so when work came to a standstill, their income stopped. With little savings, this meant that they ran out of food very quickly. Many could not afford to pay rent for the rooms they lived in. There was little support for them and so, they had no option but to find a way back to their villages where there was at least a home and the comfort of family. But most public transport had also been locked down. This forced lakhs of people to start walking. They walked for days, covering long distances. India's roads became rivers of human beings, carrying bundles and bags, often walking by night when it was cooler. Young children walked too, sometimes with family and sometimes because they were migrant workers too.

Twelve-year-old Jamlo Makdam was one such migrant worker. She belonged to the Muria community of Adivasis in Bastar, Chhattisgarh. She had gone to work in the chilli fields of Telangana with a group from her village. Children harvest chillis in these fields to provide additional livelihood for their poor families. They take home either money or sacks of chillis. Jamlo went to work sometime in February, but when the lockdown stopped work in March and the labourers had used up all their savings, they were told by their contractor to return to their villages. Jamlo and the group started walking on 16 April. They had a distance of around 200 kilometres to cover. They chose a route through the forests because the main road was locked down. They covered more than a 100 kilometres in three days. On 18 April 2020, with just 55–60 kilometres left to reach her village, Jamlo collapsed.

This book is dedicated to the memory of Jamlo. Her walk needs to be remembered if we want to create a world that shares resources fairly, a world that listens to everyone's voices, a world that is just and kind.

*Info taken from the PARI network

# Acknowledgements

My thanks are due to many people who have spent time reading the drafts of this story and talking to me as I grappled with the challenge of telling Jamlo's story, but not reducing her only to the girl who died walking. A big thank you to my grown-up readers—Anushka Ravishankar, Sayoni Basu, Usha Mukunda, Venita Coelho, Alia Sinha, Shalini Advani and Nandini Chandra—who both critiqued and encouraged, helping me clarify my intentions and writing.

Special thanks to my young readers—Aaditya, Deeya, Reyansh and Riddho—who shared their feedback with honesty and generosity. Thanks also to my editor, Smit Zaveri, who believed that this story must be shared even when I was uncertain about it. And most of all, my heartfelt gratitude to Sujata Noronha, Jamlo's champion, whose perceptive comments and firm reassurance pushed my practice. Jamlo's story, like so many stories of the lockdown, has shown us how critical it is to form community networks. And so, I feel privileged to have my community to draw upon—for feedback, critique, sustenance. Thank you, all.